What Is a Desert?

A **Just Ask** Book

Hi, my name is Christopher!

by Chris Arvetis
and Carole Palmer

illustrated by
Jim Conahan

CHILDRENS PRESS CHOICE

ISBN 0-516-09813-6

SCHOOL AND LIBRARY EDITION

A DESERT—
what's a desert?

First of all, you said it was
hot, and you're right.
No clouds are in the sky,
so the rays of the sun
are very strong.
The sun makes the desert
land very hot.

A desert is dry, too.
It does not rain often.
Some deserts go for years
without rain.
Then a heavy rainstorm
brings a lot of water
in a very short time.

A desert is windy.
The sun heats the air and causes the air to move.
The air moves so fast that it becomes a strong wind.

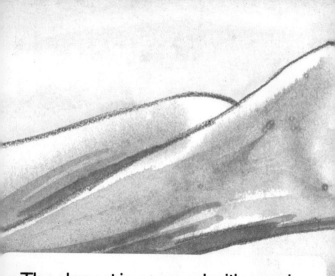

The desert is covered with sand. The wind blows the sand into hills or ridges called sand dunes.

In some deserts, there are flat-topped mountains and smaller hills.

Rainstorms make gulleys in the hills as the water runs down the steep slopes.
Soil washed down with the water forms fan-shaped ridges at the bottom.

Plants grow in the desert.
Do you know what these are?

Right, that's a cactus with
the bird peeking out.
From this palm tree
I can see sagebrush.

That tree is a Joshua tree.
Next to it is a yucca plant
growing straight up!
There are beautiful
desert flowers, too—
like these cactus flowers.

Animals live in the desert.
You know some of these animals.
There's a coyote with her pups.
And a herd of tiny mule deer.

See the mule deer
down there?

Mice, snakes, owls,
birds, scorpions,
and even turtles live
in the desert.

I know him!
Hi, Christopher!

You can even find this animal in some faraway deserts. Name this animal.

Most of all—
remember a desert is hot.
It is dry and windy.
It has lots of sand.
And many special plants
and animals live there.